POTATOES

LAKELAND

Lakeland and ACP Magazines Ltd hereby exclude all liability to the extent permitted by law for any errors or omission in this book and for any loss, damage or expense (whether direct or indirect) suffered by a third party relying on any information contained in this book.

This book was created in 2010 for Lakeland by AWW Books, an imprint of Octopus Publishing Group Ltd, based on materials licensed to it by ACP Magazines Ltd, a division of PBL Media Pty Limited.

54 Park St, Sydney
GPO Box 4088, Sydney, NSW 2001
phone (02) 9282 8618; fax (02) 9267 9438
acpbooks@acpmagazines.com.au;
www.acpbooks.com.au

OCTOPUS PUBLISHING GROUP
Design – Chris Bell
Food Director - Pamela Clark

Published for Lakeland in the United Kingdom by Octopus Publishing Group Limited

Endeavour House
189 Shaftesbury Avenue
London WC2H 8JY
United Kingdom
phone + 44 (0) 207 632 5400;
fax + 44 (0) 207 632 5405
aww@octopusbooks.co.uk;
www.octopusbooks.co.uk
www.australian-womens-weekly.com

Printed and bound in China

A catalogue record for this book is available from the British Library.

ISBN 978-1-907428-16-6

© ACP Magazines Ltd 2010
ABN 18 053 273 546

The Department of Health advises that eggs should not be consumed raw. This book contains some dishes made with raw or lightly cooked eggs. It is prudent for vulnerable people such as pregnant and nursing mothers, invalids, the elderly, babies and young children to avoid uncooked or lightly cooked dishes made with eggs. Once prepared, these dishes should be kept refrigerated and used promptly.

This book also includes dishes made with nuts and nut derivatives. It is advisable for those with known allergic reactions to nuts and nut derivatives and those who may be potentially vulnerable to these allergies, such as pregnant and nursing mothers, invalids, the elderly, babies and children to avoid dishes made with nuts and nut oils. It is also prudent to check the labels of pre-prepared ingredients for the possible inclusion of nut derivatives.

Some of the recipes in this book have appeared in other publications.

POTATOES

We've travelled the world for the 51 best-loved potato recipes, each one superbly tasty, substantial and easy to prepare. With mouthwatering salads, fritters and pancakes, soups and hearty main courses – plus step-by-step guides to perfect chips, mash, wedges and more – you'll look at the humble potato in a whole new light.

One of an exciting new series of cookbooks from Lakeland, *Potatoes* is packed with delicious colour photos and expert hints, tips and techniques for beginners and experienced cooks alike.

With every recipe triple-tested® for perfect results, these excellent cookbooks are sure to be some of the best-loved on your kitchen bookshelf. To discover the rest of the range, together with our unrivalled selection of creative kitchenware, visit one of our friendly Lakeland stores or shop online at www.lakeland.co.uk.

CONTENTS

KNOW YOUR POTATOES

POTATO VARIETIES

To ensure the best results for your potato recipe, it's important to choose a potato that is suitable. Potatoes divide into two main categories: those harvested in the spring – early or new potatoes – and those harvested in late summer or early autumn – main crop potatoes. In addition to these two categories are salad potatoes which are small and waxy. They have a similar texture to new potatoes but have a thicker skin.

The texture of potatoes varies and they are described as either waxy or floury. Waxy potatoes stay firm and are good for salads, boiling and layered potato dishes. Floury potatoes are a popular choice as they are suitable for mashing, baking, roasting and frying. They aren't, however, good for boiling as they tend to fall apart while being cooked. When buying potatoes, the description of texture and cooking qualities is your most useful guide.

There are around 80 varieties of potato available in the UK and below is a guide to the uses of just some of those most readily available:

- **Anja** Suitable for boiling and salads
- **Charlotte** Suitable for roasting, boiling, salads
- **Desiree** Suitable for baking, frying, boiling, mashing, roasting
- **Maris Bard** Suitable for boiling, frying
- **Maris Piper** Suitable for boiling, frying, baking, roasting, mashing
- **Nicola** Suitable for boiling, roasting, salads
- **Pink Fir Apple** Suitable for boiling and salads
- **Romano** Suitable for boiling, mashing, roasting, baking
- **Rooster** Suitable for frying, mashing, roasting

- **Wilja** Suitable for frying, roasting, mashing, boiling

The recipes in this book suggest which variety of potato use. If you can't find that particular variety then substitute one that has a similar texture.

STORING POTATOES

Store potatoes in a cool, dry and well ventilated place, but not in the fridge. It is particularly important to exclude light when storing potatoes to prevent the development of solanine. A high level of solanine will cause the potatoes to turn green and, as solanine is toxic, they should be discarded.

SOUPS & SALADS

VICHYSSOISE

50g butter
2 medium leeks (700g), trimmed,
  sliced thinly
750g maris piper potatoes,
  peeled, chopped coarsely
500ml chicken stock
500ml water
300ml pouring cream
2 tablespoons coarsely chopped
  fresh chives

1 Melt butter in large saucepan; cook leek, covered, about 20 minutes or until softened, stirring occasionally (do not allow leek to brown).

2 Add potato, stock and the water to pan; bring to the boil. Reduce heat; simmer, covered, until potato is tender.

3 Cool 10 minutes, then blend or process soup, in batches, until smooth; place soup in large bowl. Stir in cream, cover; refrigerate 3 hours or overnight. Divide soup among serving bowls; sprinkle with chives just before serving.

prep + cook time 1 hour 10 minutes (+ refrigeration)
serves 6
nutritional count per serving
29.2g total fat (19g saturated fat); 377 cal (1576kJ); 21.2g carbohydrate; 6.3g protein; 4.1g fibre

BACON & POTATO SOUP

6 rashers rindless bacon (390g),
   chopped coarsely
4 cloves garlic, crushed
1kg king edward potatoes,
   peeled, chopped coarsely
250ml chicken stock
500ml water
300g soured cream
3 tablespoons finely chopped
   fresh flat-leaf parsley

1 Cook bacon and garlic, stirring, in heated oiled large saucepan until bacon is crisp.
2 Add potato, stock and the water to pan; bring to the boil. Reduce heat; simmer, covered, until potato is just tender. Add soured cream; stir until heated through (do not boil). Remove from heat; stir in parsley.

prep + cook time 45 minutes
serves 6
nutritional count per serving
26.4g total fat (15.5g saturated fat); 418 cal (1747kJ); 24.1g carbohydrate; 20g protein; 3g fibre

CORN CHOWDER

40g butter
1 clove garlic, crushed
1 medium leek (350g), trimmed,
  sliced thinly
125ml dry white wine
2 stalks celery (300g), trimmed,
  chopped finely
800g desiree potatoes, peeled,
  chopped coarsely
500ml chicken stock
500ml water
320g frozen corn kernels
125ml pouring cream
1 tablespoon finely chopped fresh
  flat-leaf parsley

1 Melt butter in large saucepan;
cook garlic and leek, stirring, until
leek softens. Add wine; cook,
stirring, until liquid reduces by
half. Add celery, potato, stock
and the water; bring to the boil.
Reduce heat; simmer, covered,
until potato is just tender.
2 Cool 10 minutes, then blend
or process 750ml of the soup,
in batches, until smooth. Return
blended soup to remaining
unprocessed soup; add corn and
cream. Bring to the boil. Reduce
heat; simmer, stirring, until corn is
just tender. Remove from heat; stir
in parsley.

prep + cook time 50 minutes
serves 6
nutritional count per serving
15.8g total fat (9.8g saturated
fat); 318 cal (1329kJ); 29.7g
carbohydrate; 8g protein;
6.4g fibre

CHICKEN & WEDGES SALAD

750g king edward potatoes,
   unpeeled
1 tablespoon olive oil
4 rashers rindless bacon (260g),
   chopped coarsely
250g cherry tomatoes, halved
1 small ridged cucumber (260g),
   deseeded, sliced thinly
1 baby cos lettuce, leaves
   separated
425g coarsely chopped cooked
   chicken
herb dressing
1 tablespoon white vinegar
1 tablespoon lemon juice
1 clove garlic, crushed
80ml olive oil
2 teaspoons finely chopped fresh
   basil
2 teaspoons finely chopped fresh
   oregano

1 Preheat oven to 200°C/180°C fan-assisted. Lightly oil oven tray.
2 Cut each potato into six wedges; toss wedges in large bowl with oil. Place wedges, in single layer, on tray; roast, uncovered, about 40 minutes or until browned lightly and tender.
3 Meanwhile, cook bacon in heated oiled large frying pan, stirring, until crisp. Drain on absorbent paper.
4 Make herb dressing.
5 Combine wedges and bacon in large bowl with tomato, cucumber, lettuce and chicken. Add herb dressing; toss gently to combine.
herb dressing Combine ingredients in screw-top jar; shake well.

prep + cook time 1 hour
serves 4
nutritional count per serving
41g total fat (8.8g saturated fat); 677 cal (2830kJ); 28.2g carbohydrate; 46.4g protein; 6.4g fibre

BALSAMIC POTATO SALAD

1kg desiree potatoes, unpeeled, cut into wedges
6 spring onions, sliced thinly
35g drained sun-dried tomatoes, sliced thinly
75g pitted kalamata olives
120g soured cream
1 tablespoon balsamic vinegar
2 tablespoons milk
6 tablespoons fresh basil leaves

1 Boil, steam or microwave potato until just tender; drain. Cover; refrigerate 30 minutes.
2 Combine potato in large bowl with onion, tomato and olives.
3 To make dressing, whisk soured cream, vinegar and milk in small bowl. Pour dressing over salad; toss gently to combine, sprinkle over basil.

prep + cook time 30 minutes (+ refrigeration)
serves 4
nutritional count per serving
13.6g total fat (8.2g saturated fat); 334 cal (1396kJ); 41.3g carbohydrate; 8.5g protein; 6.3g fibre

DILL & CAPER POTATO SALAD

1kg baby new potatoes,
   unpeeled, halved
2 tablespoons white wine vinegar
125ml olive oil
½ teaspoon white sugar
1 teaspoon dijon mustard
65g rinsed drained capers
140g drained pickled cocktail
   onions, halved
200g drained cornichons, halved
   lengthways
2 tablespoons coarsely chopped
   fresh dill

1 Boil, steam or microwave potato until just tender; drain.

2 Meanwhile, to make dressing, combine vinegar, oil, sugar and mustard in screw-top jar; shake well.

3 Combine potato in large bowl with half the dressing; cool 10 minutes.

4 Add capers, onion, cornichons, dill and remaining dressing to salad; toss gently to combine.

prep + cook time 30 minutes
serves 4
nutritional count per serving
28.8g total fat (4g saturated fat);
451 cal (1885kJ); 40g carbohydrate;
6.4g protein; 5.1g fibre

CHINESE POTATO SALAD

1kg desiree potatoes, unpeeled, quartered
8 spring onions, sliced thinly
5 purple shallots, sliced thinly
6 tablespoons fresh coriander leaves
6 tablespoons coarsely chopped fresh mint
2 fresh small red thai chillies, sliced thinly
sesame lime dressing
60ml lime juice
1 egg yolk
1 teaspoon sesame oil
180ml groundnut oil
2 teaspoons mirin
2 tablespoons finely chopped fresh coriander

1 Boil, steam or microwave potato until just tender; drain.
2 Meanwhile, make sesame lime dressing.
3 Place remaining ingredients in large bowl with warm potato and sesame lime dressing; toss gently to combine.

sesame lime dressing Blend or process 1 tablespoon of the juice with egg yolk until thickened slightly. Gradually add oils in a thin, steady stream; process until mixture thickens. Stir in mirin, remaining juice and coriander.

prep + cook time 35 minutes
serves 4
nutritional count per serving
12g total fat (2.2g saturated fat); 155 cal (648kJ); 9.5g carbohydrate; 2.1g protein; 1.3g fibre
tip Purple shallots are often found under the name of thai, asian or even pink shallots; used throughout South-East Asia, they are a member of the onion family but resemble garlic in that they grow in multiple-clove bulbs and are intensely flavoured. You can substitute a small red onion instead.

SATAY CHICKEN POTATO SALAD

1kg nicola potatoes, unpeeled,
  cut into wedges
400g thinly sliced cooked chicken
6 spring onions, sliced thinly
60g baby spinach leaves, trimmed
70g roasted unsalted peanuts
150g satay sauce
120g soured cream
1 tablespoon hot water

1 Boil, steam or microwave potato until just tender; drain.
2 Combine potato in large bowl with chicken, onion, spinach and half the nuts; toss gently. Drizzle with combined remaining ingredients. Serve sprinkled with remaining nuts.

prep + cook time 35 minutes
serves 6
nutritional count per serving
26.2g total fat (10.1g saturated fat); 462 cal (1931kJ); 26.2g carbohydrate; 28g protein; 5.3g fibre

STARTERS & SNACKS

POTATO & PARSLEY WAFERS

500g maris piper potatoes,
  peeled
1 bunch fresh flat-leaf parsley
vegetable oil, for deep-frying

1 Using sharp knife, mandoline or V-slicer, cut potatoes into 2mm slices.
2 Top half of the potato slices with parsley leaves; top with remaining potato slices, press firmly to seal wafers.
3 Heat oil in large saucepan; deep-fry wafers, in batches, until browned lightly and crisp. Drain on absorbent paper.

prep + cook time 35 minutes
serves 4
nutritional count per serving
7g total fat (0.9g saturated fat); 144 cal (602kJ); 16.4g carbohydrate; 3g protein; 2g fibre
tip Try layering various herb leaves, such as sage, inside the potato wafers.

POTATO PUFFS

600g maris piper potatoes,
   peeled, chopped coarsely
50g butter, softened
1 clove garlic, crushed
3 rashers rindless bacon (195g),
   chopped finely
75g self-raising flour
1 egg, beaten lightly
2 spring onions, chopped finely
90g finely grated gruyère cheese
vegetable oil, for deep-frying

1 Boil, steam or microwave potato until tender; drain. Mash potato in medium bowl with butter and garlic until smooth; cool.

2 Meanwhile, cook bacon in oiled small frying pan until crisp; drain on absorbent paper. Add bacon, flour, egg, onion and cheese to potato mixture; stir until combined.

3 Heat oil in large deep frying pan; deep-fry level tablespoons of the potato mixture, in batches, until browned. Drain on absorbent paper. Serve with soured cream, if you like.

prep + cook time 45 minutes (+ cooling)
makes 30
nutritional count per puff
5g total fat (2g saturated fat); 76 cal (318kJ); 4.5g carbohydrate; 3g protein; 0.4g fibre

CREAMED CORN & POTATO PATTIES

800g maris piper potatoes, peeled
1 corn cob (400g), husk and silk removed
2 egg yolks
310g can creamed corn
45g fresh breadcrumbs
3 tablespoons finely chopped fresh flat-leaf parsley
35g plain flour
50g butter
60ml vegetable oil

1 Boil, steam or microwave potatoes until tender; drain.
2 Meanwhile, using sharp knife, remove kernels from corn cob.
3 Mash potatoes in large bowl until smooth. Add corn kernels, yolks, creamed corn, breadcrumbs and parsley; stir to combine.
4 Using floured hands, shape mixture into 12 patties. Toss patties in flour, shake away excess. Heat a third of the butter and 1 tablespoon of the oil in large frying pan; cook patties, four at a time, until browned both sides.
5 Repeat to make a total of 12 patties.

prep + cook time 1 hour
makes 12
nutritional count per patty
9.6g total fat (3.2g saturated fat); 194 cal (811kJ); 21g carbohydrate; 4.3g protein; 3.1g fibre

CHORIZO & POTATO FRITTERS

2 teaspoons vegetable oil
1 chorizo sausage (200g),
  chopped finely
1 small brown onion (80g),
  chopped finely
2 fresh small red thai chillies,
  chopped finely
2 medium courgettes (240g),
  grated coarsely
450g maris piper potatoes,
  peeled, grated coarsely
1 small sweet potato (250g),
  peeled, grated coarsely
3 eggs, beaten lightly
150g plain flour
1 teaspoon sweet paprika
vegetable oil, for deep-frying
sweet chilli dipping sauce
120g soured cream
2 tablespoons sweet chilli sauce

1 Heat oil in medium frying pan;
cook chorizo, onion and chilli,
stirring, until onion softens. Add
courgette; cook, stirring, 1 minute.
Cool 10 minutes.
2 Meanwhile, make sweet chilli
dipping sauce.
3 Combine chorizo mixture in
large bowl with potato, sweet
potato, eggs, flour and paprika.
4 Heat oil in large saucepan;
deep-fry level tablespoons of the
mixture, in batches, until fritters
are browned lightly. Drain on
absorbent paper. Serve with sweet
chilli dipping sauce.
sweet chilli dipping sauce
Combine ingredients in small
bowl.

prep + cook time 40 minutes
makes 40
nutritional count per fritter
4.6g total fat (1.1g saturated fat);
74 cal (309kJ); 5.3g carbohydrate;
2.6g protein; 0.6g fibre

LATKES

1kg king edward potatoes,
  peeled
1 large brown onion (200g),
  chopped finely
2 eggs, beaten lightly
55g polenta
80ml vegetable oil
100g bottled apple sauce
2 tablespoons soured cream

1 Grate potatoes coarsely; squeeze excess moisture from potato. Combine potato in large bowl with onion, egg and polenta.
2 Using floured hands, shape potato mixture into 12 rounds.
3 Heat oil in large frying pan; cook latkes, in batches, until browned lightly both sides. Drain on absorbent paper; serve topped with apple sauce and soured cream.

prep + cook time 30 minutes
makes 12
nutritional count per latke
8.5g total fat (1.9g saturated fat); 162 cal (677kJ); 16.8g carbohydrate; 3.8g protein; 1.8g fibre

tip Latkes are fried potato pancakes traditionally eaten during Hanukkah because of the significance of oil in this Jewish festival. They're generally made from matzo meal but you can substitute polenta as we have here.

SPICY POTATO PAKORAS
WITH CORIANDER RAITA

400g rooster or maris piper
   potatoes, peeled, cut into 1cm
   cubes
1 small sweet potato (250g),
   peeled, cut into 1cm cubes
1½ cups (225g) gram flour (see
   tip)
½ teaspoon bicarbonate of soda
180ml water
2 teaspoons groundnut oil
2 cloves garlic, crushed
½ teaspoon ground turmeric
1 teaspoon ground cumin
½ teaspoon dried chilli flakes
2 spring onions, chopped finely
vegetable oil, for deep-frying
coriander raita
280g greek-style yogurt
6 tablespoons coarsely chopped
   fresh coriander
1 teaspoon ground cumin

1 Make coriander raita.
2 Boil, steam or microwave potato
and sweet potato, together, until
just tender; drain. Cool 10 minutes.
3 Sift gram flour and soda into
large bowl; gradually add the
water, stirring, until batter is
smooth.
4 Heat ground nut oil in small
frying pan; cook garlic, spices and
chilli flakes, stirring, until fragrant.
Combine garlic mixture in bowl
with batter; stir in potato, sweet
potato and onion.
5 Heat vegetable oil in large
saucepan; deep-fry tablespoons
of mixture, in batches, until
pakoras are browned lightly. Drain
on absorbent paper; serve with
coriander raita.

coriander raita Combine
ingredients in small bowl.
Refrigerate until required.

prep + cook time 40 minutes
makes 24
nutritional count per pakora
4.8g total fat (1.4g saturated fat);
103 cal (430kJ); 11g carbohydrate;
3.9g protein; 1.5g fibre
tip Pakoras are small Indian fritters
that can contain vegetables, meat,
fish or rice.

GOAT'S CHEESE & POTATO FRITTERS

600g desiree potatoes, peeled,
    chopped coarsely
60ml pouring cream
¼ teaspoon ground nutmeg
3 eggs, beaten lightly
2 egg yolks, beaten lightly
75g plain flour
250g firm goat's cheese,
    crumbled
2 tablespoons coarsely chopped
    fresh flat-leaf parsley
pinch cayenne pepper
vegetable oil, for deep-frying

1 Boil, steam or microwave potatoes until tender; drain. Mash potatoes in large bowl with cream and nutmeg until smooth. Add eggs and egg yolks; using wooden spoon, beat until smooth. Stir in flour, cheese, parsley and pepper.

2 Heat oil in large saucepan; deep-fry level tablespoons of mixture, in batches, until fritters are browned lightly. Drain on absorbent paper.

prep + cook time 30 minutes
makes 32
nutritional count per fritter
5g total fat (1.9g saturated fat); 73 cal (305kJ); 4.3g carbohydrate; 2.6g protein; 0.4g fibre

POTATO BLINI WITH SALSA CRUDA

200g maris piper potatoes, peeled
110g self-raising flour
½ teaspoon bicarbonate of soda
1 teaspoon finely grated lemon rind
180ml milk
1 egg
100g butter, melted

salsa cruda
60ml lemon juice
60ml olive oil
1 clove garlic, crushed
2 medium tomatoes (380g), deseeded, chopped finely
6 tablespoons finely chopped fresh flat-leaf parsley
1 small red onion (100g), chopped finely
1 small avocado (200g), chopped finely
1 tablespoon rinsed, drained capers

horseradish topping
1 teaspoon creamed horseradish sauce
80g soured cream
¼ teaspoon sweet paprika

1 Boil, steam or microwave potatoes until tender; drain. Mash potatoes in large bowl; stir in sifted flour and soda.

2 Make a well in the centre of potato mixture; pour in combined rind, milk and egg, stirring, until batter is smooth. Cover; stand 10 minutes.

3 Make salsa cruda; make horseradish topping.

4 Heat large frying pan; brush lightly with a little of the butter. Cook tablespoons of the batter, in five batches, until browned both sides, brushing pan with butter between batches. Transfer blini to wire rack to cool. To serve, top blini with salsa cruda and horseradish topping.

salsa cruda Combine ingredients in medium bowl.

horseradish topping Combine ingredients in small bowl.

prep + cook time 1 hour
makes 25
nutritional count per blini
8.6g total fat (3.9g saturated fat); 104 cal (435kJ); 5.1g carbohydrate; 1.5g protein; 0.5g fibre

SOURED CREAM & CHIVE POTATO PANCAKES

900g maris piper potatoes,
  peeled
1 medium brown onion (150g),
  chopped finely
3 tablespoons finely chopped
  fresh chives
2 eggs, separated
2 tablespoons plain flour
120g soured cream
160ml vegetable oil
80g butter

1 Grate potatoes coarsely; squeeze excess moisture from potato with hands. Combine potato in large bowl with onion, chives, egg yolks, flour and soured cream.
2 Beat egg whites in small bowl with electric mixer until firm peaks form; gently fold into potato mixture.
3 Heat 2 tablespoons of the oil with 20g of the butter in large frying pan; cook heaped tablespoons of the potato mixture, uncovered, until browned both sides. Drain on absorbent paper; cover to keep warm.
4 Repeat to make a total of 20 pancakes. Serve with soured cream and sprinkled with chopped chives.

prep + cook time 35 minutes
makes 20
nutritional count per pancake
13.9g total fat (4.9g saturated fat); 164 cal (686kJ); 7.3g carbohydrate; 2.5g protein; 0.9g fibre
tip It is important to squeeze as much excess moisture as possible from the potato so that the pancakes hold their shape while cooking.

SPANISH TORTILLA

800g rooster or maris piper
potatoes, peeled, sliced thinly
1 tablespoon olive oil
1 large brown onion (200g), sliced
thinly
200g chorizo sausage, sliced
thinly
6 eggs, beaten lightly
300ml pouring cream
4 spring onions, sliced thickly
25g coarsely grated mozzarella
cheese
30g coarsely grated cheddar
cheese

1 Boil, steam or microwave potato until just tender; drain.

2 Meanwhile, heat oil in medium frying pan; cook brown onion, stirring, until softened. Add chorizo; cook, stirring, until crisp. Drain chorizo mixture on absorbent paper.

3 Whisk eggs in large bowl with cream, spring onion and cheeses; stir in potato and chorizo mixture.

4 Pour mixture into heated lightly oiled medium frying pan; cook, covered, over low heat, about 10 minutes or until tortilla is just set. Carefully invert tortilla onto plate, then slide back into pan; cook, uncovered, about 5 minutes or until cooked through.

prep + cook time 45 minutes
serves 4
nutritional count per serving
68.1g total fat (34.1g saturated fat); 881 cal (3683kJ); 32.6g carbohydrate; 32.7g protein; 4.1g fibre

PIROSHKI

900g plain flour
1 tablespoon dry yeast (12g)
1 tablespoon salt
75g caster sugar
2 egg yolks
500ml milk, warmed
250g butter, melted
1 egg, beaten lightly
beef filling
1 tablespoon olive oil
1 medium brown onion (150g),
    chopped finely
1 clove garlic, crushed
250g maris piper potatoes,
    peeled, chopped finely
2 rashers rindless bacon (130g),
    chopped finely
300g minced beef
90g tomato paste
2 teaspoons fresh thyme leaves

1 Combine flour, yeast, salt and sugar in large bowl. Make a well in the centre; using hands, mix in egg yolks, milk and butter until mixture is soft and elastic. Scrape down sides of bowl, cover; stand in warm place about 1 hour or until dough doubles in size.
2 Meanwhile, make beef filling.
3 Turn dough onto floured surface; knead until smooth. Divide dough into 16 pieces; press each piece into 12cm round.
4 Preheat oven to 220°C/200°C fan-assisted. Lightly oil two oven trays.
5 Place a rounded tablespoon of the beef filling in centre of each round; gather edges, pinch firmly to enclose filling. Place piroshki, pinched-side down, on prepared trays; brush with egg. Stand, uncovered, in warm place 15 minutes. Bake, uncovered, in oven about 15 minutes or until golden brown.

beef filling Heat oil in large frying pan; cook onion, garlic, potato and bacon, stirring, until potato softens. Add beef; cook, stirring, until changed in colour. Stir in paste and thyme. Cool 10 minutes.

prep + cook time 1 hour
(+ standing)
makes 16
nutritional count per piroshki
6.3g total fat (2.4g saturated fat); 322 cal (1346kJ); 49.9g carbohydrate; 14.2g protein; 2.8g fibre

tip Piroshki are small Russian dumplings that can have various savoury or sweet fillings but this one is among the most traditional. Baked or fried, they make excellent hors d'oeuvres.

WHITE FISH BRANDADE

200g maris piper potatoes,
  peeled, chopped coarsely
500ml milk
350g white fish fillets, skin and
  bones removed
80g shallots, chopped coarsely
2 cloves garlic, quartered
2 tablespoons olive oil
2 tablespoons lemon juice
60g soured cream

1 Boil, steam or microwave potato until tender; drain. Cool.
2 Meanwhile, bring milk to the boil in large frying pan; add fish, return to the boil. Reduce heat; simmer, uncovered, until fish is cooked through, turning once during cooking.
3 When fish is cool enough to handle, flake into a food processor or blender; process with potato and remaining ingredients until mixture forms a smooth paste. Place brandade in serving bowl, cover; refrigerate 30 minutes.

prep + cook time 25 minutes
(+ refrigeration)
makes 2 cups
nutritional count per tablespoon
3.7g total fat (1.5g saturated fat);
59 cal (247kJ); 2.5g carbohydrate;
4g protein; 0.2g fibre

POTATO SOUFFLÉS

350g desiree potatoes, peeled, chopped coarsely
2 tablespoons packaged breadcrumbs
60g butter
2 tablespoons plain flour
180ml milk
3 eggs, separated
90g coarsely grated cheddar cheese
1 teaspoon fresh thyme leaves

1 Boil, steam or microwave potato until tender; drain. Mash potato in large bowl.

2 Preheat oven to 200°C/180°C fan-assisted. Oil four 180ml soufflé dishes; sprinkle bases and sides with breadcrumbs, shake out excess. Place prepared dishes on oven tray.

3 Melt butter in medium saucepan; cook flour, stirring, until mixture thickens and bubbles. Gradually add milk, stirring until mixture boils and thickens; remove from heat. Stir in egg yolks, cheese, thyme and potato, mixing until cheese melts and mixture is smooth. Return soufflé mixture to same large bowl.

4 Using electric mixer, beat egg whites in small bowl until soft peaks form. Fold egg whites, in two batches, into soufflé mixture. Spoon soufflé mixture into prepared dishes; bake, uncovered, in oven about 20 minutes or until browned lightly and puffed.

prep + cook time 1 hour
serves 4
nutritional count per serving
25.9g total fat (15.3g saturated fat); 363 cal (1517kJ); 17.2g carbohydrate; 15.1g protein; 1.6g fibre

THE MAIN COURSE

PROSCIUTTO & ROAST PEPPER RÖSTI STACKS

1 small red pepper (150g)
1 small yellow pepper (150g)
90g tomato relish
1kg rooster or maris piper
    potatoes, peeled
80g unsalted butter
2 teaspoons olive oil
8 slices prosciutto (120g)
20g baby spinach leaves
50g parmesan cheese, shaved

1 Preheat grill to hot.

2 Quarter peppers; remove and discard seeds and membranes. Roast pepper under grill, skin-side up, until skin blisters and blackens. Cover pepper with plastic or paper for 5 minutes. Peel away skin, then slice pepper thinly. Combine pepper and relish in small bowl.

3 Meanwhile, grate potatoes coarsely; squeeze excess moisture from potato, then divide into eight portions.

4 Heat 10g of the butter in medium frying pan; spread one portion of the potato mixture over base of pan, flatten with spatula to form a firm pancake. Cook, uncovered, over medium heat, until golden brown on underside; shake pan to loosen rösti, then invert onto large plate. Gently slide rösti back into pan; cook, uncovered, until other side is golden brown and potato centre is tender. Drain on absorbent paper; cover to keep warm. Repeat to make a total of eight rösti.

5 Heat oil in same frying pan; cook prosciutto until crisp.

6 Place one rösti on each of four serving plates, layer with spinach, prosciutto, pepper mixture and cheese, then top with a second rösti.

prep + cook time 45 minutes
serves 4
nutritional count per serving
25.1g total fat (14.5g saturated fat); 463 cal (1935kJ); 39.3g carbohydrate; 17.7g protein; 4.9g fibre

MEDITERRANEAN POTATO PANCAKES

1 tablespoon olive oil

1 medium red onion (170g), chopped coarsely

2 cloves garlic, crushed

1 medium red pepper (200g), chopped coarsely

1 medium yellow pepper (200g), chopped coarsely

250g button mushrooms, chopped coarsely

60ml dry red wine

2 medium plum tomatoes (150g), chopped coarsely

2 x 410g cans tomatoes, crushed

200g rooster or maris piper potatoes, peeled, chopped coarsely

110g plain flour

¼ teaspoon bicarbonate of soda

2 eggs

430ml buttermilk

6 tablespoons coarsely chopped fresh basil

40g coarsely grated parmesan cheese

1 Heat oil in large frying pan; cook onion and garlic, stirring, until onion softens. Add peppers and mushroom; cook, stirring, until vegetables are just tender. Add wine, fresh tomato and 1 can of the undrained tomatoes; bring to the boil. Reduce heat; simmer, uncovered, about 10 minutes or until mixture thickens slightly.

2 Meanwhile, boil, steam or microwave potato until tender; drain. Mash potato in large bowl; cool 10 minutes.

3 Mix combined sifted flour and soda into potato; gradually whisk in combined eggs and buttermilk until batter is smooth. Refrigerate 10 minutes.

4 Preheat oven to 180°C/160°C fan-assisted.

5 Heat oiled large frying pan; cook 3 tablespoons of the batter until browned lightly both sides. Repeat to make a total of 12 pancakes. Cool pancakes 10 minutes.

6 Divide vegetable mixture among pancakes; roll to enclose filling. Place 2 pancakes, seam-side down, in each of six 375ml baking dishes.

7 Combine remaining can of undrained tomatoes and basil in small bowl; pour over pancakes, sprinkle with cheese. Bake, uncovered, in oven about 15 minutes or until heated through.

prep + cook time 1 hour 15 minutes
serves 6
nutritional count per serving
7.5g total fat (2.8g saturated fat); 256 cal (1070kJ); 30g carbohydrate; 12.6g protein; 5.3g fibre

SCALLOPED POTATOES

1.2kg desiree potatoes, peeled
150g ham, chopped finely
300ml pouring cream
180ml milk
90g coarsely grated cheddar
   cheese

1 Preheat oven to 180°C/160°C fan-assisted; oil 1.5-litre baking dish.
2 Using sharp knife, mandoline or V-slicer, slice potatoes into 2mm slices; pat dry with absorbent paper. Layer a quarter of the potato in dish; top with a third of the ham. Continue layering remaining potato and ham, finishing with potato.
3 Heat cream and milk in small saucepan until almost boiling; pour over potato mixture. Cover with foil; bake in oven 30 minutes. Remove foil; bake 20 minutes. Top with cheese; bake, uncovered, about 20 minutes or until potato is tender. Stand 10 minutes before serving.

prep + cook time 1 hour 30 minutes
serves 6
nutritional count per serving
29.5g total fat (18.8g saturated fat); 446 cal (1864kJ); 29.1g carbohydrate; 15.2g protein; 3.2g fibre

PORTUGUESE POTATOES

600g maris piper potatoes,
    peeled, chopped coarsely
2 tablespoons olive oil
2 cloves garlic, crushed
1 large brown onion (200g),
    chopped coarsely
4 medium tomatoes (760g),
    chopped coarsely
2 teaspoons sweet paprika
2 teaspoons finely chopped fresh
    thyme
125ml chicken stock
1 tablespoon peri-peri sauce
1 tablespoon coarsely chopped
    fresh flat-leaf parsley

1 Preheat oven to 220°C/200°C fan-assisted.
2 Toss potato and half the oil in medium shallow baking dish. Roast, uncovered, about 30 minutes or until browned lightly.
3 Meanwhile, heat remaining oil in large frying pan; cook garlic and onion, stirring, until onion softens. Add tomato, paprika and thyme to pan; cook, stirring, about 1 minute or until tomato just softens. Add stock and sauce to pan; bring to the boil. Reduce heat; simmer, uncovered, stirring occasionally, about 10 minutes or until sauce thickens slightly.
4 Remove potato from oven; reduce oven temperature to 180°C/160°C fan-assisted.
5 Pour sauce over potato; bake, uncovered, about 20 minutes or until potato is tender. Serve sprinkled with parsley.

prep + cook time 1 hour 10 minutes
serves 6
nutritional count per serving 6.5g total fat (0.9g saturated fat); 157 cal (656kJ); 18.2g carbohydrate; 4.5g protein; 3.9g fibre

COTTAGE PIE

1 tablespoon olive oil
2 cloves garlic, crushed
1 large brown onion (200g),
 chopped finely
2 medium carrots (240g), peeled,
 chopped finely
1kg minced beef
1 tablespoon worcestershire
 sauce
2 tablespoons tomato paste
2 x 425g cans tomatoes, crushed
1 teaspoon dried mixed herbs
200g button mushrooms,
 quartered
120g frozen peas
1kg maris piper potatoes, peeled,
 chopped coarsely
180ml hot milk
40g butter, softened
50g grated cheddar cheese

1 Heat oil in large saucepan; cook garlic, onion and carrot, stirring, until onion softens. Add beef; cook, stirring, about 10 minutes or until changed in colour.
2 Add sauce, paste, undrained tomatoes and herbs to pan; bring to the boil. Reduce heat; simmer, uncovered, about 30 minutes or until mixture thickens slightly. Stir in mushrooms and peas.
3 Preheat oven to 180°C/160°C fan-assisted.
4 Meanwhile, boil, steam or microwave potato until tender; drain. Mash potato in large bowl with milk and butter.
5 Pour beef mixture into deep 3-litre ovenproof dish; top with mashed potato mixture, sprinkle with cheese. Bake, uncovered, in oven about 35 minutes or until pie is heated through and top is browned lightly.

prep + cook time 2 hours
serves 8
nutritional count per serving
20.7g total fat (9.5g saturated fat); 432 cal (1806kJ); 26.3g carbohydrate; 32.2g protein; 6.2g fibre

SMOKED FISH POT PIES

750g smoked cod fillets
500ml milk
1 bay leaf
6 black peppercorns
1kg maris piper potatoes, peeled,
    chopped coarsely
50g butter, softened
20g butter, extra
1 large brown onion (200g),
    chopped finely
1 clove garlic, crushed
35g plain flour
625ml milk, extra
120g frozen peas
1 teaspoon finely grated lemon
    rind
2 tablespoons lemon juice
2 hard-boiled eggs, quartered

1 Place fish, milk, bay leaf and peppercorns in medium saucepan; bring to the boil. Reduce heat; simmer, uncovered, 10 minutes. Drain; discard liquid and spices. Remove and discard skin from fish; flake flesh into large chunks in medium bowl.

2 Meanwhile, boil, steam or microwave potato until tender; drain. Mash potato with softened butter in large bowl; cover to keep warm.

3 Melt extra butter in medium saucepan; cook onion and garlic, stirring, until onion softens. Add flour; cook, stirring, until mixture thickens and bubbles. Gradually add extra milk; stir until mixture boils and thickens. Add peas, rind and juice; remove from heat. Stir in fish.

4 Divide egg, fish mixture and potato mixture among four 500ml flameproof dishes. Place dishes on oven tray under very hot grill until tops are browned lightly.

prep + cook time 1 hour
serves 4
nutritional count per serving
30.4g total fat (18.1g saturated fat); 756 cal (3160kJ); 58.8g carbohydrate; 57.7g protein; 6.8g fibre

MASH-FILLED CABBAGE ROLLS WITH CHEESY CREAM SAUCE

1kg maris piper potatoes, peeled, chopped coarsely
40g butter, softened
1 egg yolk
4 large cabbage leaves
4 rashers rindless bacon (260g), chopped coarsely
30g coarsely grated cheddar cheese

cheesy cream sauce
20g butter
35g plain flour
375ml chicken stock
125ml pouring cream
60g coarsely grated cheddar cheese
3 tablespoons finely chopped fresh flat-leaf parsley

1 Boil, steam or microwave potato until tender; drain. Mash potato in large bowl with butter and egg yolk.
2 Meanwhile, discard thick stems from cabbage. Boil, steam or microwave leaves until just pliable; drain. Rinse under cold water; drain. Pat dry with absorbent paper.
3 Preheat oven to 200°C/180°C fan-assisted. Make cheesy cream sauce.
4 Place leaves, vein-side up, on board. Cut leaves in half lengthways; divide potato mixture evenly among leaf halves, placing mixture at stem end. Roll firmly, folding in sides to enclose filling.
5 Place cabbage rolls, seam-side down, in shallow lightly oiled 2-litre ovenproof dish; pour cheesy cream sauce over rolls, sprinkle with bacon and cheese. Bake, uncovered, in oven about 20 minutes or until bacon is crisp and cabbage rolls are heated through.

cheesy cream sauce Melt butter in medium saucepan, add flour; cook, stirring, until mixture thickens and bubbles. Gradually add stock and cream; stir until mixture boils and thickens. Stir in cheese and parsley.

prep + cook time 1 hour
serves 4
nutritional count per serving
41.8g total fat (24.8g saturated fat); 671 cal (2805kJ); 41.9g carbohydrate; 30g protein; 5.5g fibre

STUFFED PORTOBELLO MUSHROOMS

500g desiree potatoes, peeled,
  chopped coarsely
60ml hot pouring cream
20g butter, softened
8 large portobello mushrooms
  (400g)
30g butter, melted, extra
1 tablespoon olive oil
1 small brown onion (80g),
  chopped finely
2 cloves garlic, crushed
1 fresh small red thai chilli,
  chopped finely
120g coarsely grated cheddar
  cheese
3 tablespoons coarsely chopped
  fresh flat-leaf parsley
2 tablespoons finely chopped
  fresh chives
1 teaspoon fresh thyme leaves

1 Preheat oven to 180°C/160°C fan-assisted.

2 Boil, steam or microwave potato until tender; drain. Mash potato in large bowl with cream and softened butter. Cover to keep warm.

3 Meanwhile, remove and reserve stems from mushrooms. Brush caps with extra butter; place, stem-side up, on oven tray. Bake, uncovered, in oven 5 minutes; cover to keep warm.

4 Chop reserved stems finely. Heat oil in medium frying pan; cook onion, garlic, chilli and mushroom stems, stirring, until onion softens. Add cheese, parsley, chives and thyme; stir until combined.

5 Combine onion mixture with potato mixture; spoon mixture into mushroom caps.

6 Place caps on oven tray under hot grill about 5 minutes or until browned lightly.

prep + cook time 40 minutes
serves 4
nutritional count per serving
31g total fat (18.1g saturated fat); 428 cal (1789kJ); 18.5g carbohydrate; 15g protein; 5.1g fibre

VEGETARIAN POTATO TARTS

1kg desiree potatoes, peeled, chopped coarsely
125ml hot vegetable stock
30g butter
2 cloves garlic, crushed
200g mushrooms, sliced thickly
2 tablespoons finely shredded fresh basil
2 spring onions, chopped finely
80g coarsely grated cheddar cheese
3 sheets filo pastry
30g butter, melted

1 Boil, steam or microwave potato until tender; drain. Mash potato in large bowl with stock.

2 Meanwhile, melt butter in small frying pan; cook garlic and mushroom, stirring, until mushroom softens. Stir mushroom mixture, basil, onion and half the cheese into potato mixture.

3 Preheat oven to 200°C/180°C fan-assisted. Oil four 250ml metal pie dishes. Place a 2.5cm x 30cm strip of baking parchment over base of each dish, extending 5cm over sides of dishes.

4 Stack filo sheets; cut stack in half crossways. Brush between layers with melted butter, then cut stack into four squares. Line prepared dishes with squares. Spoon potato mixture into dishes; sprinkle with remaining cheese.

5 Place dishes on oven tray; bake tarts in oven about 15 minutes or until pastry is browned lightly. Use baking parchment strips to lift tarts out of dishes.

prep + cook time 45 minutes
serves 4
nutritional count per serving
19.9g total fat (12.5g saturated fat); 406 cal (1697kJ); 39.3g carbohydrate; 14.5g protein; 5.9g fibre

POTATO DUMPLINGS WITH BURNT BUTTER

1kg charlotte potatoes, unpeeled
1 clove garlic, crushed
50g butter, softened
2 eggs, beaten lightly
100g plain flour
20g finely grated parmesan
    cheese
500ml water
1 litre chicken stock
125g butter, chopped
3 tablespoons fresh sage leaves
1 teaspoon lemon juice

1 Boil, steam or microwave potatoes until tender; drain. When cool enough to handle, peel potatoes. Mash in large bowl with garlic and softened butter. Mix in egg, flour and cheese, stirring, until mixture forms a soft dough.
2 Bring the water and stock to the boil in large saucepan. Reduce heat; cook rounded tablespoons of the dough, in batches, in simmering stock mixture about 4 minutes or until dumplings rise to the surface. Using slotted spoon, remove dumplings; divide dumplings among serving bowls.
3 Meanwhile, melt chopped butter in small frying pan; when butter just sizzles, cook sage until crisp, drain on absorbent paper. Reheat butter in same pan; stir over low heat until just browned. Remove from heat; stir in juice. Drizzle dumplings with burnt butter; top with crisp sage leaves.

prep + cook time 1 hour 15 minutes
serves 4
nutritional count per serving
41.7g total fat (26g saturated fat); 662 cal (2767kJ); 53g carbohydrate; 17g protein; 5.1g fibre

BUBBLE & SQUEAK

450g nadine potatoes, peeled,
   chopped coarsely
250g cabbage, chopped coarsely
4 rashers rindless bacon (260g),
   chopped coarsely
1 medium brown onion (150g),
   chopped coarsely

1 Boil, steam or microwave potato and cabbage, separately, until just tender; drain. Mash potato in medium bowl until smooth.
2 Meanwhile, cook bacon in heated large frying pan, stirring, until crisp; drain on absorbent paper.
3 Cook onion in pan, stirring, until softened. Add potato, cabbage and bacon; stir to combine. Flatten mixture to form large cake-shape; cook, uncovered, until bottom of potato cake is just browned. Carefully invert onto plate, then slide back into frying pan; cook, uncovered, until browned on other side.

prep + cook time 40 minutes
serves 4
nutritional count per serving
6.4g total fat (2.3g saturated fat); 216 cal (903kJ); 18.7g carbohydrate; 18.4g protein; 4.5g fibre

tip Originally made from the leftovers of a roast dinner, usually cabbage, potatoes and, if any remained, meat. Bubble and squeak's name is supposedly derived from the sounds the ingredients make while being tossed together in a frying pan.

SMOKED SALMON PIE

1kg charlotte potatoes, peeled,
  chopped coarsely
40g butter, softened
60g soured cream
200g smoked salmon, chopped
  coarsely
2 eggs, separated
2 spring onions, chopped finely

1 Preheat oven to 200°C/180°C fan-assisted.
2 Boil, steam or microwave potato until tender; drain. Mash potato in large bowl with butter and soured cream. Stir in salmon, one of the egg yolks, egg whites and onion.
3 Spoon mixture into oiled deep 22cm-round ovenproof dish; smooth top with spatula, brush with remaining egg yolk. Bake, uncovered, in oven, about 25 minutes or until pie is heated through and browned lightly.

prep + cook time 45 minutes
serves 6
nutritional count per serving 12.9g total fat (7g saturated fat); 268 cal (1120kJ); 22.4g carbohydrate; 14.2g protein; 2.7g fibre

CHORIZO-STUFFED POTATOES

8 maris piper potatoes (960g), unpeeled
1 teaspoon olive oil
70g chorizo sausage, chopped finely
1 clove garlic, crushed
250g canned tomatoes, crushed
90g soured cream
2 tablespoons grated mozzarella cheese

1 Preheat oven to 200°C/180°C fan-assisted. Lightly oil oven tray.
2 Boil, steam or microwave potatoes until tender; drain.
3 Meanwhile, heat oil in small frying pan; cook chorizo, stirring, about 3 minutes or until crisp. Drain on absorbent paper. Cook garlic in same pan, stirring over low heat, until just fragrant. Return chorizo to pan with undrained tomatoes; simmer, uncovered, until mixture reduces by half.
4 Cut shallow slice from top of each potato; using teaspoon, scoop flesh from each top into medium bowl, discard skin. Using teaspoon, carefully scoop about two-thirds of the flesh from each potato into same bowl; reserve potato shells.
5 Mash potato until smooth; stir in chorizo mixture and soured cream. Place potato shells on prepared tray. Divide mixture among potato shells, sprinkle with cheese; bake, uncovered, in oven about 15 minutes or until heated through.

prep + cook time 45 minutes
serves 4
nutritional count per serving
17.1g total fat (8.5g saturated fat); 349 cal (1459kJ) ; 34.4g carbohydrate; 11g protein; 5.7g fibre

ALOO GOBI

450g maris piper potatoes,
  peeled, chopped coarsely
20g ghee
1 tablespoon black mustard seeds
1 tablespoon cumin seeds
3 cloves garlic, crushed
½ teaspoon ground turmeric
½ teaspoon garam masala
1 large brown onion (200g), sliced
  thinly
2 medium tomatoes (380g),
  chopped coarsely
1kg cauliflower, chopped coarsely
250ml water
3 tablespoons fresh coriander
  leaves

1 Boil, steam or microwave potato until just tender; drain.

2 Meanwhile, melt ghee in large saucepan; cook seeds, stirring, until they begin to pop. Add garlic, turmeric and garam masala; cook, stirring, until mixture is fragrant. Add onion; cook, stirring, until onion softens. Add tomato and cauliflower; cook, stirring, 1 minute.

3 Stir in the water; bring to the boil. Reduce heat; simmer, covered, 10 minutes. Stir in potato; simmer, covered, about 5 minutes or until vegetables are tender. Remove from heat; stir in coriander.

prep + cook time 45 minutes
serves 4
nutritional count per serving
5.2g total fat (2.9g saturated fat); 203 cal (849kJ); 24.8g carbohydrate; 10.1g protein; 8.5g fibre

ROSEMARY & POTATO PIZZA

3 medium desiree potatoes
  (630g), unpeeled
1 teaspoon fresh rosemary leaves
2 tablespoons olive oil
150g self-raising flour
150g plain flour
30g butter
1 egg, beaten lightly
80ml milk
40g finely grated parmesan
  cheese
2 cloves garlic, crushed

1 Peel and coarsely chop one of the potatoes; boil, steam or microwave until tender, drain. Mash in small bowl; reserve ½ cup mashed potato.

2 Using sharp knife, mandoline or V-slicer, slice remaining potatoes into 2mm slices. Pat dry with absorbent paper. Combine sliced potato in medium bowl with rosemary and oil.

3 Preheat oven to 200°C/180°C fan-assisted. Lightly oil 25cm x 30cm swiss roll tin.

4 Combine flours in large bowl; using fingertips, rub butter into flour until mixture resembles fine breadcrumbs. Add mashed potato, egg and milk; stir until combined. Turn dough onto floured surface; knead until smooth.

5 Roll dough into 25cm x 30cm rectangle; carefully lift onto prepared tin. Using palm of hand, press dough into corners of tin to ensure base is covered evenly. Top with cheese and garlic; layer potato slices, overlapping slightly, over dough. Bake, uncovered, in oven about 30 minutes or until potato is tender and pizza is browned lightly.

prep + cook time 1 hour
serves 8
nutritional count per serving
10.8g total fat (4.2g saturated fat); 291 cal (1216kJ); 37.6g carbohydrate; 8.9g protein; 3.1g fibre

ROAST POTATO & BACON QUICHE

300g maris piper potatoes,
  peeled, chopped coarsely
1 tablespoon olive oil
1 sheet ready-rolled puff pastry,
  thawed
2 teaspoons olive oil, extra
1 small brown onion (80g), sliced
  thinly
2 cloves garlic, crushed
3 rashers rindless bacon (195g),
  chopped coarsely
80ml milk
80ml pouring cream
2 eggs
25g coarsely grated mozzarella
  cheese

1 Preheat oven to 180°C/160°C fan-assisted.

2 Place potato and oil in medium baking dish; stir to coat potato with oil. Roast, uncovered, about 30 minutes or until browned lightly and cooked through.

3 Meanwhile, cut pastry into four squares; gently press one square into each of four 250ml ovenproof dishes, lightly prick pastry with fork. Place dishes on oven tray; bake in oven 5 minutes.

4 Reduce oven temperature to 160°C/140°C fan-assisted.

5 Heat extra oil in medium frying pan; cook onion, garlic and bacon, stirring, until onion softens and bacon is crisp. Drain on absorbent paper.

6 Divide potato among pastry shells; top with bacon mixture. Pour combined milk, cream, eggs and cheese over bacon mixture Bake, uncovered, in oven about 25 minutes or until quiche filling sets. Stand 5 minutes; carefully remove quiches from dishes.

prep + cook time 1 hour 25 minutes
serves 4
nutritional count per serving
34.5g total fat (15.7g saturated fat); 509 cal (2128kJ); 27.8g carbohydrate; 21.2g protein; 2.3g fibre

SIDE DISHES

POTATOES ANNA

1.2kg maris piper potatoes,
   peeled
100g butter, melted

1 Preheat oven to 240°C/220°C fan-assisted. Lightly oil shallow 2-litre 26cm-round baking dish.
2 Using sharp knife, mandoline or V-slicer, slice potatoes into 2mm slices; pat dry with absorbent paper. Place a single layer of potato, slightly overlapping, into baking dish; brush with a little of the butter. Continue layering remaining potato and butter, cover dish with foil; bake 20 minutes.
3 Remove foil; use metal spatula to press down on potato.
4 Reduce oven temperature to 220°C/200°C fan-assisted; bake, uncovered, about 30 minutes or until top is crisp and browned lightly. Cut into wedges to serve.

prep + cook time 1 hour 10 minutes
serves 6
nutritional count per serving 13.9g total fat (9g saturated fat); 255 cal (1066kJ); 26.3g carbohydrate; 4.9g protein; 3.2g fibre

LAYERED POTATOES

500g maris piper potatoes,
  unpeeled
100g butter, melted
2 cloves garlic, crushed
60g finely grated parmesan
  cheese
6 spring onions, sliced thinly
6 tablespoons coarsely chopped
  fresh flat-leaf parsley

1 Preheat oven to 200°C/180°C fan-assisted. Line bases of four 250ml metal moulds or ovenproof baking dishes with baking parchment.
2 Using sharp knife, mandoline or V-slicer, slice potatoes into 2mm slices; pat dry with absorbent paper. Place a few potato slices in each mould, dot with a little of the combined butter and garlic, cheese, onion and parsley. Continue layering remaining ingredients, finishing with potato; cover each mould with foil, place on oven tray. Bake in oven about 30 minutes or until potato is tender. Stand 5 minutes before turning out.

prep + cook time 1 hour
serves 4
nutritional count per serving
25.6g total fat (16.6g saturated fat); 340 cal (1421kJ); 17.4g carbohydrate; 9.2g protein; 3.1g fibre

COTTAGE FRIES

1kg maris piper potatoes,
  peeled
30g butter, chopped
125ml vegetable oil
1 medium brown onion (150g),
  sliced thickly

1 Using sharp knife, mandoline or V-slicer, slice potatoes into 2mm slices. Stand potato slices in large bowl of cold water for 30 minutes to avoid discolouration. Drain; pat dry with absorbent paper.

2 Heat a third of the butter and a third of the oil in large frying pan; cook a third of the potato and a third of the onion, stirring occasionally, until browned lightly and cooked through. Drain on absorbent paper; cover to keep warm. Repeat, making two more batches, with remaining butter, oil, potato and onion. Return cottage fries to pan; toss to combine, season with freshly cracked black pepper and sea salt, if desired.

prep + cook time 20 minutes (+ standing)
serves 4
nutritional count per serving 35.2g total fat (7.7g saturated fat); 488 cal (2040kJ); 34.8g carbohydrate; 6.6g protein; 4.5g fibre

HASH BROWNS

1kg maris piper potatoes, unpeeled
1 small brown onion (80g), chopped finely
2 teaspoons finely chopped fresh rosemary
60g ghee

1 Boil, steam or microwave unpeeled potatoes until just tender; drain. Cool 10 minutes.
2 Peel potatoes; cut into 1cm cubes. Combine potato in large bowl with onion and rosemary.
3 Heat a third of the ghee in medium heavy-based frying pan; place four egg rings in pan. Spoon 3 tablespoons of the potato mixture into each egg ring; using spatula, spread mixture evenly to fill ring. Cook, pressing frequently with spatula, until browned underneath; carefully turn each ring to brown other side. Drain on absorbent paper; cover to keep warm.
4 Repeat to make a total of 12 hash browns.

prep + cook time 40 minutes
makes 12
nutritional count per hash brown
5.1g total fat (3.3g saturated fat); 103 cal (431kJ); 11.3g carbohydrate; 2.1g protein; 1.8g fibre
tips A mixture of half olive oil and half melted butter can be used instead of ghee. Originally called 'hashed brown potatoes', this popular American dish can be eaten at breakfast, lunch or dinner.

FENNEL & POTATO GRATIN

800g maris piper potatoes, peeled
2 small fennel bulbs (400g), sliced thinly
1 tablespoon plain flour
430ml pouring cream
60ml milk
20g butter, chopped
90g coarsely grated cheddar cheese
50g stale breadcrumbs

1 Preheat oven to 180°C/160°C fan-assisted; oil deep 2-litre baking dish.

2 Using sharp knife, mandoline or V-slicer, slice potatoes into 2mm slices; pat dry with absorbent paper. Layer a quarter of the potato slices into baking dish; top with a third of the fennel. Continue layering remaining potato and fennel, finishing with potato.

3 Blend flour with a little of the cream in medium jug to form a smooth paste; stir in remaining cream and milk. Pour cream mixture over potato; dot with butter. Cover with foil; bake in oven about 1 hour or until vegetables are just tender. Remove foil, top with combined cheese and breadcrumbs; bake, uncovered, about 15 minutes or until top is browned lightly.

prep + cook time 1 hour 35 minutes
serves 8
nutritional count per serving 29.7g total fat (19.4g saturated fat); 391 cal (1634kJ); 21.7g carbohydrate; 8.1g protein; 3.4g fibre

MASHED POTATO CASSEROLE

500g maris piper potatoes,
  peeled, chopped coarsely
30g butter, softened
2 eggs, beaten lightly
300ml pouring cream
120g coarsely grated cheddar
  cheese
2 tablespoons coarsely chopped
  fresh chives

1 Boil, steam or microwave potato until tender; drain. Mash potato in large bowl with butter until smooth; spread over base of lightly oiled shallow 1.5-litre baking dish.
2 Preheat oven to 180°C/160°C fan-assisted.
3 Combine remaining ingredients in medium bowl; pour over potato. Bake, uncovered, about 40 minutes or until top sets and is browned.

prep + cook time 1 hour 10 minutes
serves 4
nutritional count per serving
51.5g total fat (32.7g saturated fat); 597 cal (2495kJ); 18.7g carbohydrate; 15.4g protein; 2g fibre

SKORDALIA

400g rooster or maris piper
  potatoes, peeled, chopped
  coarsely
2 slices white bread
60g ground almonds
3 cloves garlic, crushed
2 tablespoons cider vinegar
80ml water
60ml olive oil

1 Boil, steam or microwave potato until tender; drain. Mash potato in medium bowl.

2 Meanwhile, trim and discard crusts from bread. Soak bread in small bowl of cold water; drain. Squeeze out excess water.

3 Blend or process bread with ground almonds, garlic, vinegar and the water until mixture is smooth. With motor operating, gradually add oil in a thin steady stream, processing until mixture thickens slightly. Fold bread mixture into potato mash.

prep + cook time 30 minutes
makes 2 cups
nutritional count per tablespoon
3.7g total fat (0.4g saturated fat); 52 cal (217kJ); 3.2g carbohydrate; 1.1g protein; 0.6g fibre
tip Skordalia is a tangy Greek sauce or dip made with puréed potatoes and breadcrumbs or ground nuts (or, as in this case, both). Skordalia can be served with almost any kind of dish – from grilled meats and poultry to fish and raw vegetables.

COLCANNON

1kg maris piper potatoes, peeled, chopped coarsely
80ml hot pouring cream
80g butter, softened
2 medium brown onions (300g), chopped finely
1 clove garlic, crushed
350g savoy cabbage, shredded finely

1 Boil, steam or microwave potato until tender; drain. Mash potato, cream and half the butter in medium bowl until mixture is smooth.
2 Melt remaining butter in large frying pan; cook onion and garlic, stirring, until onion softens. Add cabbage; cook, stirring, about 2 minutes or until cabbage just wilts. Gently fold potato mixture into cabbage mixture.

prep + cook time 35 minutes
serves 4
nutritional count per serving 25.5g total fat (16.5g saturated fat); 439 cal (1835kJ); 39.9g carbohydrate; 8.9g protein; 8.3g fibre
tip Colcannon is a traditional Irish dish made with mashed potato and cabbage or kale.

DUCHESSE POTATOES

1kg nicola potatoes, peeled,
    chopped coarsely
3 egg yolks
100g butter, melted

1 Preheat oven to 180°C/160°C
fan-assisted; oil and line two oven
trays with baking parchment.
2 Boil, steam or microwave potato
until tender; drain. Mash potato
in large bowl with egg yolks and
butter.
3 Spoon potato mixture into
large piping bag fitted with a
1cm-fluted tube; pipe potato into
3cm rosette-shaped swirls onto
oven trays.
4 Bake, uncovered, in oven
about 30 minutes or until browned
lightly.

prep + cook time 1 hour
makes 40
nutritional count per rosette
2.5g total fat (1.5g saturated fat);
40 cal (167kJ); 3.3g carbohydrate;
0.8g protein; 0.4g fibre

SPECIAL-OCCASION MASH

1kg maris piper potatoes, peeled,
   chopped coarsely
250g mascarpone cheese
80g finely grated parmesan
   cheese
80g finely grated mozzarella
   cheese
125ml hot milk

1 Boil, steam or microwave potato
until tender; drain. Mash potato
in large bowl with remaining
ingredients.

prep + cook time 30 minutes
serves 4
nutritional count per serving
48.1g total fat (31.3g saturated
fat); 661 cal (2763kJ); 35.4g
carbohydrate; 20.7g protein;
4g fibre

POTATO, OLIVE & SUN-DRIED TOMATO BREAD

250g maris piper potatoes,
  peeled, chopped coarsely
30g butter, melted
300g self-raising flour
250ml milk
60g pitted green olives, sliced
  thickly
75g drained sun-dried tomatoes
  in oil, sliced thickly
100g coarsely grated mozzarella
  cheese

1 Preheat oven to 200°C/180°C fan-assisted. Oil 14cm x 21cm loaf tin; line base and sides with baking parchment, extending paper 5cm over long sides.
2 Boil, steam or microwave potato until tender; drain. Mash potato in large bowl with butter until smooth.
3 Add flour, milk, olives, tomato and cheese to potato mixture; mix to combine. Spoon into prepared tin; bake, uncovered, in oven about 50 minutes or until cooked through.

prep + cook time 1 hour 15 minutes
serves 8
nutritional count per serving
8.3g total fat (4.8g saturated fat); 262 cal (1095kJ); 35.3g carbohydrate; 9.8g protein; 3.3g fibre

BOXTY

900g nadine potatoes, peeled
100g butter
1 clove garlic, crushed
450g self-raising flour
1 tablespoon milk
2 teaspoons sesame seeds

1 Boil, steam or microwave half of the potatoes; drain. Mash cooked potatoes in large bowl until smooth. Coarsely grate remaining raw potatoes.
2 Preheat oven to 180°C/160°C fan-assisted. Line two oven trays with baking parchment.
3 Add butter, garlic, flour and grated potato to mashed potato; stir until mixture forms a dough.
4 Knead dough on lightly floured surface; divide into quarters. Using hands, shape each quarter into 20cm round; score a shallow cross into top of each round.
5 Place rounds on trays; brush with milk, sprinkle evenly with sesame seeds. Bake, uncovered, in oven 20 minutes. Cover with foil; bake a further 20 minutes or until cooked through.

prep + cook time 1 hour 15 minutes
serves 4
nutritional count per serving
23.1g total fat (14g saturated fat); 733 cal (3064kJ); 109.3g carbohydrate; 17.1g protein; 8.1g fibre
tip Believed to have originated during the Irish famine, boxty is made of a mixture of mashed and grated potato and shaped into a thick pancake.

PERFECT POTATOES

PERFECT MASH

1kg desiree potatoes, peeled,
   cut into 3cm pieces
40g butter, softened
180ml hot milk

1 Place potato in medium pan with enough cold water to barely cover. Boil, uncovered, over medium heat about 15 minutes or until potato is tender. Drain.
2 Using the back of a wooden spoon, push potato through fine sieve into large bowl. Use spoon to stir butter and hot milk into potato, folding gently until mash is smooth and fluffy.

prep + cook time 30 minutes
serves 4
nutritional count per serving
10.2g total fat (6.6g saturated fat); 271 cal (1133kJ); 35g carbohydrate; 7.6g protein; 4g fibre
tips Mash the potato in a bowl with a traditional potato masher. Don't try to mash potato in a food processor as it will become gluey. After potato is drained, work quickly, never allowing it to become cold. Heat any liquid ingredients you intend to stir into the mash. Different potato varieties absorb different amounts

of water when cooked, and the method of cooking (steaming, microwaving or boiling) also determines how much water is absorbed into the cooked potato. The age of the potato also has an effect on the amount of liquid it can absorb, therefore, the amount of liquid needed for a perfect mash will vary. With practice, you should be able to tell by looking at a mash mixture when it has had the right amount of liquid added.

Use a wooden spoon to push the potato through a fine sieve.

A potato ricer is great when making small amounts of mash.

A food mill (mouli) will also ensure the mash is lump-free.

PERFECT POTATO CRUSH

1kg baby new potatoes,
  unpeeled
120g soured cream
40g butter, softened

1 Boil, steam or microwave whole potatoes until tender; drain.
2 Mash about half the unpeeled whole potatoes, soured cream and butter in large bowl until smooth; stir in one of the flavour variations.
3 Using back of a fork or potato masher, gently crush remaining potatoes until skins burst and flesh is just flattened; fold into mash mixture.

prep + cook time 20 minutes, depending on the flavour used.
serves 4
nutritional count per serving
20.4g total fat (13.2g saturated fat); 354 cal (1480kJ); 33.7g carbohydrate; 6.8g protein; 5g fibre

FLAVOUR VARIATIONS
original potato salad Combine 6 coarsely chopped drained cornichons, 3 coarsely chopped spring onions, 3 tablespoons coarsely chopped fresh flat-leaf parsley and 1 tablespoon coarsely chopped rinsed drained capers.

caesar salad Fry 3 finely chopped bacon slices until crisp; drain on absorbent paper. Combine with 4 finely chopped anchovies, 1 crushed garlic clove, 3 thinly sliced spring onions and 40g shaved parmesan cheese.

herb & mustard salad Combine 1 tablespoon wholegrain mustard, 3 tablespoons each coarsely chopped fresh chives and coarsely chopped fresh flat-leaf parsley and 2 tablespoons each coarsely chopped fresh basil and coarsely chopped fresh dill.

Mash half of the potatoes with the sour cream and butter in a large bowl.

Once the potato mash is smooth, stir in one of the flavour variations.

Gently crush the remaining potatoes until skins burst and flesh is just flattened.

THE PERFECT POTATO CHIP

1kg maris piper potatoes, peeled
ground nut oil, for deep-frying

1 Cut potatoes lengthways
into 1cm slices; cut each slice
lengthways into 1cm-wide pieces.
Stand potato pieces in large bowl
of cold water for 30 minutes to
avoid discolouration. Drain; pat
dry with absorbent paper.

2 Heat oil in deep-fryer or large
saucepan; cook chips, in three
batches, about 4 minutes each or
until just tender but not browned.
Drain on absorbent paper; stand
10 minutes.
3 Reheat oil; cook chips, in three
batches, separating any that stick
together by shaking deep-fryer
basket or with a slotted spoon,
until crisp and golden brown.
Drain on absorbent paper.

prep + cook time 30 minutes
serves 4
nutritional count per serving
14g total fat (2.5g saturated
fat); 289 cal (1208kJ); 32.8g
carbohydrate; 6g protein; 4g fibre
tips After the first cooking, the
chips can stand for several hours
before the final deep-frying. Corn
oil or vegetable oil can also be
used.

Cut the potatoes into 1cm slices,
then cut each slice into 1cm-wide
pieces; place into cold water.

After the first frying, the chips
should be tender, but not brown;
drain chips on absorbent paper.

After the second frying, the chips
should be crisp and golden brown
in colour.

PERFECT POTATO SKINS

1kg desiree potatoes, unpeeled
2 tablespoons olive oil

1 Preheat oven to 220°C/200°C fan-assisted.
2 Scrub potatoes well; brush with half the oil. Place potatoes on oven tray; bake, uncovered, about 50 minutes or until tender. Cool.
3 Cut each potato into six wedges; carefully remove flesh, leaving skins intact. Place potato skins, skin-side down, on wire rack over oven tray; brush with remaining oil. Roast, uncovered, about 20 minutes or until crisp.

prep + cook time 1 hour 15 minutes (+ cooling)
serves 4
nutritional count per serving
9.4g total fat (1.3g saturated fat); 249 cal (1041kJ); 32.8g carbohydrate; 6g protein; 5g fibre

DIPS
horseradish & soured cream
Combine 1 finely chopped small brown onion, 3 tablespoons creamed horseradish sauce, 180ml soured cream, ¼ teaspoon sweet paprika and 60ml cream in bowl.

hummus Blend or process 300g can rinsed drained chickpeas, 2 tablespoons lemon juice, 1 crushed garlic clove, 60ml olive oil, 2 tablespoons tahini and 2 tablespoons water until almost smooth.

tapenade Blend or process 2 tablespoons roasted pine nuts, 300g pitted black olives, 1 crushed garlic clove, 1 tablespoon lemon juice, 1 drained anchovy fillet and 60ml olive oil until almost smooth.

Carefully scoop out the flesh from the wedges, leaving the skins intact.

Place the potato skins on a wire rack over an oven tray, then brush with the oil.

Hot, crisp potato skins are delicious with the dip of your choice.

PERFECT POTATO WEDGES

1kg kipfler potatoes, unpeeled, washed
2 tablespoons olive oil

1 Preheat oven to 200°C/180°C fan-assisted. Lightly oil two oven trays.
2 Cut each potato into wedges; toss potato wedges and oil in large bowl. Place wedges, in single layer, on trays; roast, uncovered, turning occasionally, about 40 minutes or until crisp and cooked through.

prep + cook time 50 minutes
serves 4
nutritional count per serving
9.4g total fat (1.3g saturated fat); 249 cal (1044kJ); 32.8g carbohydrate; 6g protein; 5g fibre
tip Any waxy salad potato can be used for this recipe.

SPICE FLAVOURINGS
lemon pepper Combine 1 tablespoon finely grated lemon rind, 1 tablespoon lemon juice and ½ teaspoon freshly ground black pepper in small bowl.

sun-dried tomato flavouring
Combine 1 tablespoon sun-dried tomato pesto, 2 teaspoons tomato sauce and 1 teaspoon sambal oelek in small bowl.

cajun pepper Combine ½ teaspoon ground oregano, 2 teaspoons ground cumin, 1 teaspoon hot paprika, ½ teaspoon ground black pepper, 1 teaspoon ground turmeric, 1 teaspoon ground coriander and ¼ teaspoon chilli powder in small bowl.

Wedges can be coated in egg white rather than oil for a lower-fat version.

Add your choice of spice to the wedges, then bake, in a single layer, on lightly oiled oven trays.

PERFECT SAUTÉED POTATOES

1kg desiree potatoes, unpeeled
2 tablespoons olive oil
50g butter, chopped

1 Cut potatoes into 1cm slices.
2 Heat oil and butter in large frying pan; cook potato, covered, over medium heat, turning occasionally, until browned lightly. Reduce heat; cook, tossing pan to turn potato slices, about 10 minutes or until tender.

prep + cook time 25 minutes
serves 4
nutritional count per serving
19.6g total fat (8g saturated fat); 339 cal (1419kJ); 32.8g carbohydrate; 6.1g protein; 4g fibre

Using a sharp knife, cut the unpeeled potatoes into 1cm slices.

Melt the chopped butter with the oil in a large frying pan over medium heat.

Toss the potato slices in the frying pan until they are cooked through.

PERFECT RÖSTI

1kg rooster or maris piper
   potatoes, peeled
1 teaspoon salt
80g unsalted butter
2 tablespoons vegetable oil

1 Grate potatoes coarsely into
large bowl, stir in salt; squeeze
excess moisture from potatoes.
Divide potato mixture into eight
portions.

2 Heat 10g of the butter and
1 teaspoon of the oil in medium
frying pan; spread one portion of
the potato mixture over base of
pan, flatten with spatula or egg
slice to form a firm pancake.
3 Cook, uncovered, over medium
heat, until golden brown on
underside; shake pan to loosen
rösti, then invert onto a large
plate. Gently slide rösti back into
pan; cook, uncovered, until other
side is golden brown and potato
centre is tender.

5 Drain on absorbent paper;
cover to keep warm.
4 Repeat to make a total of eight
rösti.

prep + cook time 25 minutes
makes 8
nutritional count per rösti
13g total fat (6.1g saturated
fat); 198 cal (828kJ); 16.4g
carbohydrate; 3.1g protein;
2g fibre

Coarsely grate the potatoes into
a large bowl; add the salt to draw
out any excess liquid.

Flatten the potato mixture with a
spatula or egg slice to form a firm
round pancake.

Invert the rösti onto a large plate,
then gently slide it back into the
pan; cook until browned lightly.

GLOSSARY

bicarbonate of soda also called baking soda; used as a leavening agent in baking.

black mustard seeds also known as brown mustard seeds.

breadcrumbs

packaged fine-textured, purchased white breadcrumbs.

stale one- or two-day-old bread made into crumbs by grating, blending or processing.

buttermilk originally the term given to the slightly sour liquid left after butter was churned from cream, today it is made similarly to yogurt. Sold alongside fresh milk products in supermarkets. Despite the implication of its name, it is low in fat.

capers the grey-green buds of a warm climate shrub sold either dried and salted or pickled in vinegar brine.

cayenne pepper thin-fleshed, long, very-hot red chilli; usually purchased dried and ground.

cheese

cheddar the most common cow's milk cheese; should be aged and hard.

goat's made from goat's milk, goat's cheese has an earthy, strong taste. Can be purchased in both soft and firm textures, in various shapes and sizes, sometimes rolled in ash or herbs.

Available from most supermarkets and delicatessens.

gruyère A firm, cows' milk Swiss cheese having small holes and a nutty, slightly salty flavour. Emmental or appenzeller can be used as a substitute. Available at most supermarkets and delicatessens.

mascarpone a cultured cream product made in much the same way as yogurt. It's whitish to creamy yellow in colour, with a soft, creamy texture.

mozzarella a semi-soft cheese with a delicate, fresh taste; has a low melting point and stringy texture when hot.

parmesan a sharp-tasting, dry, hard cheese, made from skimmed or semi-skimmed milk and aged for at least a year.

chorizo a sausage of Spanish origin; made of coarsely ground pork and seasoned with garlic and chillies.

cornichon French for gherkin, a very small variety of cucumber, often pickled

cream we used fresh cream in this book, unless otherwise stated. Also known as pure cream and pouring cream; has no additives unlike commercially thickened cream. Minimum fat content 35%.

soured a thick commercially-cultured soured cream. Minimum fat content 35%.

fennel bulb vegetable, also known as finocchio or anise. Also the name given to dried seeds having a liquorice flavour.

filo pastry chilled or frozen tissue-thin pastry sheets that are very versatile, lending themselves to both sweet and savoury dishes.

flour

gram a fine, powdery flour made from dried, ground chickpeas; used in India for making various breads. Available from health food stores and supermarkets.

plain all-purpose flour.

self-raising plain flour sifted with baking powder (a raising agent consisting mainly of 2 parts cream of tartar to 1 part bicarbonate of soda) in the proportion of 150g flour to 2 level teaspoons baking powder.

garam masala a blend of spices based on varying proportions of cardamom, cinnamon, cloves, coriander, fennel and cumin, roasted and ground together. Black pepper and chilli can be added for a hotter version.

ghee clarified butter; with the milk solids removed, this fat can be heated to a very high temperature without burning.

greek-style yogurt a full-cream yogurt, often made from sheep's milk; its thick, smooth consistency, almost like whipped cream, is attained by draining off the milk liquids.

mirin sweet low-alcohol rice wine used in Japanese cooking.

mustard

dijon a pale brown, distinctively flavoured fairly mild French mustard.

wholegrain also known as seeded. A French-style coarse-grain mustard made from crushed mustard seeds and dijon-style French mustard.

olives

black have a richer and more mellow flavour than the green ones and are softer in texture. Sold either plain or in a piquant marinade.

green those harvested before fully ripened and are, as a rule, denser and more bitter than their black relatives.

onions

brown an all-purpose onion, with a light brown skin and yellow flesh.

red a sweet-flavoured, large, purple-red onion.

white has a creamy white flesh and a papery white skin. Their pungent flesh adds flavour to a vast range of dishes.

paprika ground dried red bell pepper; available in sweet, smoked or hot varieties. Sweet paprika is available at delis, speciality food stores and on line.

polenta a flour-like cereal made from ground corn; similar to cornmeal but finer and lighter in colour; also the name of the dish made from it.

portabello mushrooms mature chestnut mushrooms. Large, dark brown mushrooms with full-bodied flavour; ideal for filling or barbecuing.

prosciutto salted-cured, air-dried (unsmoked), pressed ham; usually sold in paper-thin slices, ready to eat.

raita a cooling side dish made from yogurt, cucumber and spices.

sambal oelek Indonesian in origin; a salty paste made from ground chillies and vinegar. Available in Asian food stores and supermarkets.

sauces

peri-peri a hot, fragrant sauce used in both Portuguese and African cuisines.

sweet chilli a comparatively mild, Thai-type sauce made from red chillies, sugar, garlic and vinegar.

satay spicy sauce made from peanuts.

worcestershire a dark-brown spicy sauce used to season meat, gravies and cocktails, and as a condiment.

sesame seeds black and white are the most common of these tiny oval seeds; a good source of calcium.

sun-dried tomatoes dried tomatoes sometimes bottled in oil.

sun-dried tomato pesto a sauce of sun-dried tomatoes blended with herbs, pine nuts, garlic, vinegar, olive oil, parmesan and sometimes red wine.

tomato paste a triple-concentrated tomato purée used to flavour soups, stews, sauces and casseroles.

vinegar

balsamic authentic only from the province of Modena, Italy; made from a regional wine of white trebbiano grapes specially processed then aged in antique wooden casks to give the exquisite pungent flavour.

cider a vinegar made from fermented apples.

white wine based on fermented white wine.

yeast we used dried yeast; allow 15g compressed yeast to each 2 teaspoons (7g) dried yeast if substituting.

INDEX

CONVERSION CHARTS

measures

One metric tablespoon holds 20ml; one metric teaspoon holds 5ml.

All cup and spoon measurements are level. The most accurate way of measuring dry ingredients is to weigh them. When measuring liquids, use a clear glass or plastic jug with metric markings.

We use large eggs with an average weight of 60g.

dry measures

METRIC	IMPERIAL
15g	½oz
30g	1oz
60g	2oz
90g	3oz
125g	4oz (¼lb)
155g	5oz
185g	6oz
220g	7oz
250g	8oz (½lb)
280g	9oz
315g	10oz
345g	11oz
375g	12oz (¾lb)
410g	13oz
440g	14oz
470g	15oz
500g	16oz (1lb)
750g	24oz (1½lb)
1kg	32oz (2lb)

liquid measures

METRIC	IMPERIAL
30ml	1 fluid oz
60ml	2 fluid oz
100ml	3 fluid oz
125ml	4 fluid oz
150ml	5 fluid oz
190ml	6 fluid oz
250ml	8 fluid oz
300ml	10 fluid oz
500ml	16 fluid oz
600ml	20 fluid oz
1000ml (1 litre)	32 fluid oz

length measures

3mm	⅛in
6mm	¼in
1cm	½in
2cm	¾in
2.5cm	1in
5cm	2in
6cm	2½in
8cm	3in
10cm	4in
13cm	5in
15cm	6in
18cm	7in
20cm	8in
23cm	9in
25cm	10in
28cm	11in
30cm	12in (1ft)

oven temperatures

These are fan-assisted temperatures. If you have a conventional oven (ie. not fan-assisted), increase temperatures by 10–20°.

	°C (CELSIUS)	°F (FAHRENHEIT)	GAS MARK
Very low	100	210	½
Low	130	260	1–2
Moderately low	140	280	3
Moderate	160	325	4–5
Moderately hot	180	350	6
Hot	200	400	7–8
Very hot	220	425	9